Coping *with* Emotional & Physical Pain *workbook*

Facilitator Reproducible Guided Self-Exploration Activities

Ester R.A. Leutenberg
& John J. Liptak, EdD

Illustrated by Amy L. Brodsky, LISW-S

Duluth, Minnesota

Whole Person
210 West Michigan Street
Duluth, MN 55802-1908

800-247-6789

books@wholeperson.com
www.wholeperson.com

Coping with Emotional & Physical Pain Workbook
Facilitator Reproducible Guided Self-Exploration Activities

Printed in the United States of America

10 9 8 7 6 5 4 3 2 1

Editorial Director: Carlene Sippola
Art Director: Joy Morgan Dey

Library of Congress Control Number: 2013936570
ISBN: 978-157025-299-0

Using this Book

Pain is an inevitable part of everyone's life, and the effective management of pain is critical in people's life satisfaction and general well-being. **Physical pain** is any pain experienced in the body signaling something wrong in the body and needing to be fixed. **Emotional pain** is the feelings associated with an emotional trauma either from the past or present.

Both physical pain and emotional pain have potential to cause considerable problems in a person's life. Both types of pain must be explored and managed in order for people to live satisfying and healthy lives. Sometimes emotional issues manifest as physical discomfort; often physical pain leads to emotional suffering.

Emotional Pain

All people, at some time in their lives, struggle to overcome emotional pain. Emotional pain resulting from a past trauma might be caused by events in childhood such as neglect, abuse, abandonment, changes in a family structure and/or loss of parent. Emotional pain resulting from a trauma in the present might be caused from events as the end of a relationship, loss of a loved one, unemployment, divorce or separation, crime, rape, terrorist threat/event, and/or returning from war.

Emotional pain can affect relationships, personal lives, professional careers and general life satisfaction and physical health. Symptoms of emotional pain:

- Aggressive behavior
- Changed sleeping patterns
- Difficulty letting go of painful memories
- Difficulty managing angry feelings
- Disturbing sudden mental images
- Feeling of hopelessness
- Feelings of guilt
- Inability to forgive self or others
- Inability to stop dwelling on past events
- Lack of energy
- Recurring nightmares
- Reliving a painful event over and over
- Repression or denial of events
- Sadness and depression
- Self-destructive behaviors such as substance abuse
- Sense of worthlessness

Depending on the severity of a person's emotional pain, treatment may take several forms including behavior modification and psychological counseling. In order to cope with emotional pain, one needs to enhance positive emotions and face and release negative emotions. This workbook is designed to help your participants with this coping process.

This book is not intended to be a substitution for medical treatment by a qualified physician.

Physical Pain

Physical pain is the body's way of alerting us that something is wrong. Feelings of pain vary from person to person. There are basically two types of pain.

- **Acute pain** is a sudden and unusual mild or acute pain in the body. This pain may last for weeks or months. Examples of acute pain include broken bones, burns, cuts and childbirth. Unrelieved acute pain may lead to chronic pain.
- **Chronic pain** continues even after an injury has healed. This pain can last for weeks, months or years and can include tense muscles, limited mobility and nerve damage that affect a person's ability to engage in normal work, leisure or community activities. Examples of chronic pain include migraine headaches, lower and upper back pain, arthritis and nerve damage. Chronic pain can originate from an injury, trauma, infection or other conditions.

Typical Pain Treatments

Depending on the severity of pain, the treatment can take various forms:

- Acupuncture
- Biofeedback
- Chiropractic Sessions
- Drug Treatment
- Nerve Blocks
- Physical Therapy
- Surgery
- Other alternative modalities

While these forms of therapy may be effective, many people continue to live with chronic physical pain. For these people it is important and helpful to learn techniques to manage their pain effectively. The *Coping with Emotional & Physical Pain Workbook* provides assessments and self-guided activities to help participants learn useful skills for coping with various forms of emotional and physical pain.

A variety of self-exploration activities is provided for participants to determine which best suit their unique needs.

Format of Book

The *Coping with Emotional & Physical Pain Workbook* contains assessments and guided self-exploration activities that can be used with a variety of populations to help participants cope more effectively with the various types of pain in their lives. Each chapter of this workbook begins with an annotated Table of Contents with notes and examples for the facilitator. Each chapter contains two primary elements: 1) A set of assessments to help participants gather information about themselves in a focused situation, and 2) a set of guided self-exploration activities to help participants process information and learn ways of coping with emotional and physical pain.

Assessments

Each chapter begins with an assessment that provides participants with valuable information about themselves. These assessments help participants identify productive and unproductive patterns of behavior and life skills and guide participants' awareness of how they interact with the world. Assessments provide a path to self-discovery through the participants' exploration of their own unique traits and behaviors. The purpose of these assessments is not to "pigeon-hole" people, but to allow them to explore various elements that are critical for coping with emotional and physical pain. This book contains *self-assessments* and not *tests*. Traditional tests measure knowledge or right or wrong responses. For the assessments provided in this book, remind participants that there are no right or wrong answers. These assessments ask only for opinions or attitudes about topics related to a variety of coping skills and abilities.

Assessments in this book are based on self-reported data. In other words, the accuracy and usefulness of the information is dependent on the information that participants honestly provide about themselves. All of the assessments in this workbook are designed to be administered, scored, and interpreted by the participants as a starting point for them to begin to learn more about themselves and their coping skills. Remind participants that the assessments are exploratory exercises and not a determination of abilities. Lastly, the assessments are not a substitute for professional assistance. If you feel any of your participants need more assistance than you can provide, please refer them to an appropriate professional.

As your participants begin the assessments in this workbook give these instructions:

Take your time. Because there is no time limit for completing the assessments, work at your own pace. Allow yourself time to reflect on your results and how they compare to what you already know about yourself.

- Do not answer the assessments as you think others would like you to answer them or how you think others see you. These assessments are for you to reflect on your life and explore some of the barriers keeping you from managing the emotional and physical pain in your life.
- Assessments are powerful tools if you are honest with yourself. Take your time and be truthful in your responses so that your results are an accurate reflection of *you*. Your level of commitment to seeing yourself clearly will determine how much you learn about yourself.
- Before completing each assessment, be sure to read the instructions. The assessments have similar formats, but they have different scales, responses, scoring instructions and methods for interpretation.
- Finally, remember that learning about yourself should be a positive and motivating experience. Don't stress about taking the assessments or discovering your results. Just respond honestly and learn as much about yourself as you can.

(Continued on the next page)

Format of Book *(Continued)*

Guided Self-Exploration Activities

Guided self-exploration activities are any exercises that assist participants in self-reflection and enhance self-knowledge, identify potential ineffective behaviors, and teach more effective ways of coping. Guided self-exploration is designed to help participants make a series of discoveries that lead to increased social and emotional competencies, as well as to serve as an energizing way to help participants grow personally and professionally. These brief, easy-to-use self-reflection tools are designed to promote insight and self-growth. Many different types of guided self-exploration activities are provided for you to pick and chose the activities most needed and/or will be most appealing to the participants. The unique features of self-guided exploration activities make them usable and appropriate for a variety of individual sessions and group sessions.

Features of Guided Self-Exploration Activities

- **Quick, easy and rewarding to use** – These guided self-exploration activities are designed to be an efficient, appealing method for motivating participants to explore information about themselves – including their thoughts, feelings, and behaviors – in a relatively short period of time.
- **Reproducible** – Because the guided self-exploration activities can be reproduced by the facilitator, no more than the one book needs to be purchased. You may photocopy as many items as you wish for your participants. If you want to add or delete words on a page, make one photocopy, white out and/or write your own words, and then make photocopies from your personalized master.
- **Participative** – These guided self-exploration activities help people to quickly focus their attention in the self-reflection process and to learn new and more effective ways of coping.
- **Motivating to complete** – The guided self-exploration activities are designed to be an energizing way for participants to engage in self-reflection and learn about themselves. Various activities are included to enhance the learning process related to developing important social and emotional competency skills.
- **Low risk** – The guided self-exploration activities are designed to be less risky than formal assessments and structured exercises. They are user-friendly, and participants will generally feel rewarded and motivated after completing these activities.
- **Adaptable to a variety of populations** – The guided self-exploration activities can be used with many different populations and can be tailored to meet the needs of the specific populations with whom you work.
- **Focused** – Each guided self-exploration activity is designed to focus on a single coping issue, thus enhancing the experience for participants.
- **Flexible** – The guided self-exploration activities are flexible and can be used independently or to supplement other types of interventions.

Note to Facilitators

For most of the activities contained in this book, the authors have provided one set of reproducible sheets for reflection and journaling. Participants may need multiple copies based on the number types of emotional and physical pain they are experiencing. For example, a participant who has both back pain and shoulder pain may need two sets of copies of each of the activities to complete. Please feel free to photocopy as many pages as necessary.

Chapter Elements

The Coping with Emotional & Physical Pain Workbook is designed to be used either independently or as part of an integrated curriculum. You may administer any of the assessments and the guided self-exploration activities to an individual or a group with whom you are working, and you may administer any of the activities over one or more days. Feel free to pick and choose those assessments and activities that best fit the outcomes you desire.

The first page of each chapter begins with an annotated Table of Contents with notes and examples for the facilitator.

Assessments – Assessments with scoring directions and interpretation materials begin each chapter. The authors recommend that you begin presenting each topic by asking participants to complete the assessment. Facilitators can choose one or more, or all of the activities relevant to their participants' specific needs and concerns.

Guided Self-Exploration Activities – Practical questions and activities to prompt self-reflection and promote self-understanding are included after each of the assessments. These questions and activities foster introspection and promote pro-social behaviors and coping skills. The activities in this workbook are tied to the assessments so that you can identify and select activities quickly and easily.

The activities are divided into four chapters to help you identify and select assessments easily and quickly:

Chapter 1: Types of Emotional Pain
This chapter helps participants explore the various types of emotional pain they may be experiencing.

Chapter 2: Coping With Emotional Pain
This chapter helps participants identify their emotional pain coping skills.

Chapter 3: Level of Physical Pain
This chapter helps participants explore the level of their physical pain.

Chapter 4: Pain Management
This chapter helps participants identify how effectively they are managing the physical pain they are experiencing.

Thanks to . . .

Amy Brodsky, illustrator extraordinaire,

and to the following professionals whose input in this book has been invaluable!

Carol Butler, MS Ed, RN, C

Jay Leutenberg

Kathy Liptak, Ed.D.

Eileen Regen, M.Ed., CJE

Table of Contents

Types of Emotional Pain

Coping with Emotional Pain

Table of Contents *(continued)*

Types of Emotional Pain

Table of Contents and Facilitator Notes

Participants will be asked to identify current connections and how they nurture them.

My Current Connections	How They Nurture Me
EX: The mountains.	*When I see the mountains I feel safe and the beauty warms my heart.*

Participants will be asked to list words or phrases that describe them.
Example: Fun-loving, cranky.

Activities I LIKE to Do by Myself	Activities I THINK I Can Do by Myself I Would Like to Try
EX: Read a good book.	*I'll go to a movie myself that no one else wants to see.*

Aspects of My Life	With Whom Can I Connect?	How I Can Connect
EX: Community	*The American Cancer Society*	*Walk in the Relay for Life and raise money.*

Bring to the session: magazines, art supplies, quotations, crayons, highlighters and paste or glue.

Prior to beginning the session, ask if the participants exercise by walking. Brainstorm together ways they can find time to walk and where they can walk.

Try some laughter therapy with the group. Ask if there's anyone who can stand up and start laughing. Encourage the group to join in.

Person	How this Person Exhibits Hopefulness	How I Can Spend Time with this Person
EX: Suzie	*Always sees the silver lining.*	*Call her and invite her to lunch at my house.*

Table of Contents and Facilitator Notes

Types of Emotional Pain Scale Introduction and Directions

Name ______________________________________ Date _______________

Emotional pain can be described as feelings resulting from difficult, frightening or painful experiences. Many different emotions cause pain. The purpose of this assessment is to help you identify your level of pain in five common areas of emotional pain.

The Types of Emotional Pain Scale is designed to help you understand any areas in which you are experiencing emotional pain.

This scale contains 30 statements. Read each statement and decide whether it is true or false for you. If the statement is true, circle the number under the TRUE column. If the statement is false, circle the number under the FALSE column.

	TRUE	FALSE
I feel as if I'm outside looking in	(2)	1

In the above statement, the circled 2 means that the statement is true for the person completing the assessment.

This is not a test and there are no right or wrong answers. Do not spend too much time thinking about your answers. Your initial response will be the most true for you. Be sure to respond to every statement.

Turn to the next page and begin.

Types of Emotional Pain Scale

	TRUE	FALSE
I feel as if I'm outside looking in	2	1
I feel invisible.	2	1
I find it painful to be alone.	2	1
I hunger for close friendships or a closer family group	2	1
I have no one to ask for emotional support.	2	1
I feel easily rejected in social situations..	2	1

SECTION I TOTAL = __________

	TRUE	FALSE
I feel down in the dumps a lot.	2	1
I am usually negative.	2	1
I want to sleep a lot..	2	1
It is hard for me to experience pleasure	2	1
I often feel worthless and hopeless.	2	1
I constantly feel as if I'm going uphill.	2	1

SECTION II TOTAL = __________

	TRUE	FALSE
I become angry when little things go wrong	2	1
I am frequently irritable and argumentative.	2	1
I have a difficult time controlling my anger.	2	1
I hurt other people when I feel hurt.	2	1
I say things I regret when I'm angry.	2	1
I hold on to my resentments..	2	1

SECTION III TOTAL = __________

Continued on the next page

Types of Emotional Pain Scale *(Continued)*

	TRUE	FALSE
I often feel frustrated..	2	1
I make small problems into large ones and then become anxious.	2	1
I worry about things that others do not worry about.	2	1
I am anxious about the least little thing.	2	1
I can't stop worrying, even when I try.	2	1
I will look to find things to worry about.	2	1

SECTION IV TOTAL = ________

	TRUE	FALSE
I enjoy putting others down.	2	1
I often think others are better off than I am.	2	1
I resent others who I think have more than I do..	2	1
I feel relieved when others do not get more than I do.	2	1
I see my friends as rivals.	2	1
I am sad when others have more than I do..	2	1

SECTION V TOTAL = ________

Go to the Scoring Directions on the next page

Types of Emotional Pain Scale Scoring Directions

The *Types of Emotional Pain Scale* is designed to measure the emotional pain you are feeling in life. Add the numbers you've circled for each of the five sections on the previous pages. Put that total on the line marked TOTAL at the end of each section.

Then, transfer your totals for each of the five sections to the lines below:

SECTION I TOTAL = __________ Loneliness

SECTION II TOTAL = __________ Sadness

SECTION III TOTAL = __________ Anger

SECTION IV TOTAL = __________ Anxiety and Worry

SECTION V TOTAL = __________ Jealousy

Profile Interpretation

Individual Scale Score	Result	Indications
6 to 7	low	If you scored in the low range on any of the scales, you are probably not experiencing much emotional pain in your life.
8 to 10	moderate	If you scored in the moderate range on any of the scales, you are probably experiencing some emotional pain in your life.
11 to 12	high	If you scored in the high range on any of the scales, you are probably experiencing a great deal of emotional pain in your life.

Types of Emotional Pain
Scale Descriptions

Following are scale descriptions for the assessment you completed. After you explore the areas in which you scored in the moderate or high levels, you will have activities and exercises to help you better manage your emotional pain.

LONELINESS: People scoring high on this scale have few supportive or nurturing relationships in their lives. They feel a disconnection that keeps them emotionally isolated when they do not want to be. They long for a significant other, good friends, family and a sense of community.

SADNESS: People scoring high on this scale are unable to enjoy life because they feel despondent. They find it difficult to experience much pleasure, and they experience prolonged periods of feeling down, sad, pessimistic and self-critical. They may feel fatigued and uninterested in engaging in activities.

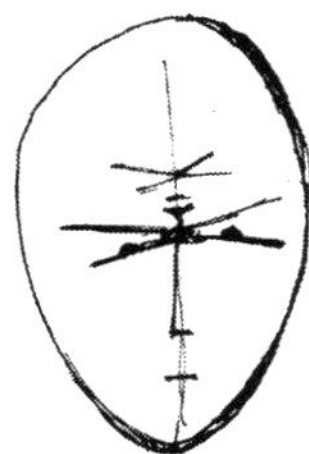

ANGER: People scoring high on this scale feel strong displeasure that arises when a need is not met or an expectation is not fulfilled. Sometimes anger arises for no good reason at all. These people may have a difficult time dealing with their anger and they often do things while angry that they regret later.

ANXIETY and WORRY: People scoring high on this scale tend to worry a lot. They feel an intensified emotional response to some sort of fear, whether this fear is imagined or real. They tend to be unable to find a sense of calm and well-being. They experience anxiety and may even have full-blown panic attacks.

JEALOUSY: People scoring high on this scale tend to become jealous of other people. They may feel as if they do not measure up to others or get their due. They do not want the best for others because it makes them feel unworthy and unappreciated. They may unconsciously put others down to defend their own self-image.

Acknowledge your Current Connections

It's important to acknowledge the supportive relationships you have already developed. These connections are not always with people; they may be with animals, nature or a spiritual being. In the spaces below, identify your current connections and how they nurture you.

My Current Connections	How They Nurture My Commonalities

Commonalities

It's important to meet people who have characteristics similar to yours. How would you describe yourself? In the spaces that follow, list words or phrase that describe you.

____

____

____

____

____

____

____

Where can you go to meet people and spend time with people like yourself?

____

____

____

____

Alone Time

Connecting with yourself can allow you to be aware that you are always with someone wonderful – YOURSELF! By tuning in to yourself, you will realize that you are never alone. What types of activities do you like to do by yourself, and which might you like to try?

Activities I LIKE to Do By Myself	Activities I THINK I Can Do by Myself I Would Like to Try

Connecting with Others

Connecting with others can diminish your social isolation. You can explore many ways to overcome social isolation and connect with other people. Think about how you can overcome your social isolation in various aspects of your life.

Aspects of My Life	With Whom Can I Connect?	How I Can Connect?
Community		
Spirituality		
Work		
Leisure/Friendships		
Other		

Relationship Qualities I Cherish

In the space below, identify the types of relationship characteristics you desire (sense of humor, quiet, etc.). You can write the words in colors, highlighters or fancy lettering. You can also cut out and glue magazine pictures or words in the space provided.

Now, where can you meet people who have these characteristics?

____

____

Walking

SADNESS

Rather than staying home and allowing the endless negative thoughts to continue playing in your mind, you should try and get moving. Exercise begins a cycle of igniting and increasing serotonin (serotonin is a hormone that is naturally found in the human brain and is referred to as the "happy" hormone because it greatly enhances your overall well-being, regulates your mood and relieves feelings of depression) and energy, enhancing your self-image, and improving sleep. Start slowly with gentle walking and then you can expand your walking routine.

My Walking Routine

Day and Date	Distance Walked	How I Felt After

Laughter

Laughter can be great medicine for people who are depressed. Laughter increases the levels of your endorphins (a substance in the brain that is released to diminish all sensations of pain), reduces stress, and raises your spirits. Check what types of activities you find humorous and respond to the questions.

❑ Watch funny movies or videos. What are your favorites? ______________________

____

❑ Read funny books. What kind do you like?

❑ Surround yourself with humorous people. Who are they and how do they show their humor? ______________________

____

❑ Be around upbeat people. Who are they and how do they show their positivity? ______

____

❑ Enjoy comedians. Who are your favorites and why? ______________________

____

❑ Others ______________________________________

____

Hopeful People

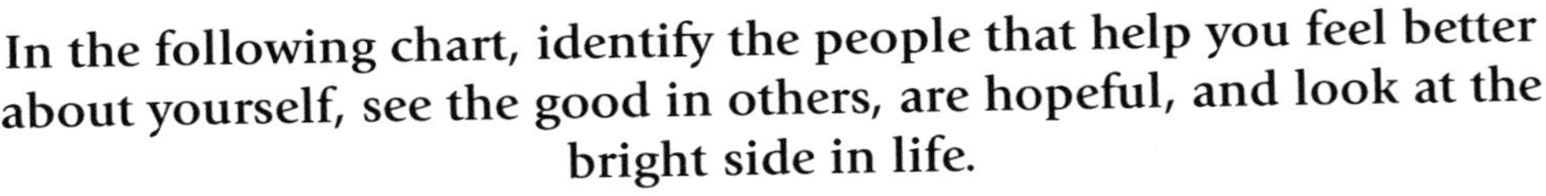
In the following chart, identify the people that help you feel better about yourself, see the good in others, are hopeful, and look at the bright side in life.

Person	How this Person Exhibits Hopefulness	How I Can Spend Time with this Person

Hopeful Situations

In the following chart, identify the situations that help you feel better about yourself, give you a glimmer of hopefulness, and allow you to look at the bright side in life.

Situation	How this Situation Promotes Hopefulness	How I Can Spend More Time at It

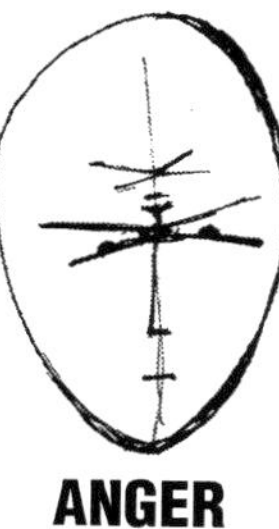

My Anger Log

It is important for people suffering from emotional pain to identify what is happening when anger erupts. This will provide clues to your anger's source(s). The following anger log will help you keep track of the thoughts, feelings, and behaviors related to your angry feelings. You can think back to times when you were angry and complete the following log, or you can keep it with you this week and make note of when you get angry and what is happening when you feel angry.

Place and Situation________________________ Date and Time__________

Describe what was happening when you got angry. ____________________

____

____

How did your body change? ________________________________

____

____

How did you try to calm your body? ___________________________

____

____

What thoughts triggered the anger? ___________________________

____

____

How did you try to redirect your thinking? ______________________

____

____

How did you overcome your angry feelings?______________________

____

____

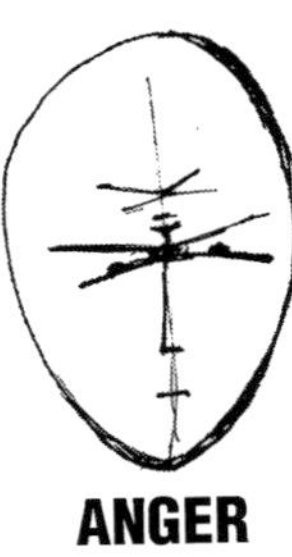

Write a Letter

One of the values of writing a letter is that as you put your angry thoughts on paper, you sort them out in your mind. You can write things you want to say to another person. Afterwards, you can read it over and choose whether to keep it for a while and then reread it, mail it, tear it up, or tell the person.

Who is causing you emotional pain because of some trauma the person caused you?

____

What did this person do to cause you emotional pain?

____

____

Write a letter to this person and express your anger for what the person did.

Dear______________,

____

____

____

____

____

____

____

____

____

____

____

____

____

____

____

Your Thoughts

ANXIETY and WORRY

Your thoughts have a huge influence on the amount of anxiety that you feel. It may help you to change your thinking. Think about a situation in which you feel anxious. Then identify the thoughts that keep running through your head related to this situation.

In what situation do you feel very anxious?

____

____

What negative thoughts go through your mind about this situation?

____

____

What positive thoughts could you use to replace those negative thoughts?

____

____

Stay in the Now

It is important to stop projecting your anxiety into the future. Rather, you need to stay in the present. When anxious thoughts begin to take you into the future, try to bring your attention back to the NOW. Say things to yourself like:

"Today I will feel good!"

"Today I appreciate what I have."

"Right now, I am enjoying the bright, sunny day."

Write your thoughts in the spaces that follow:

____

____

____

____

____

Situations I Usually Worry About

Identify five situations that you tend to worry about. These situations could occur at home, work, during your leisure time, or in relationships, your immediate community or the global community.

Situation	My Worry	Is there anything I can do about it? If so, what? If not, write a calming thought about this situation.
1) Home		
2) Work		
3) Leisure Time		
4) Relationships		
5) Community		
Other		
Other		

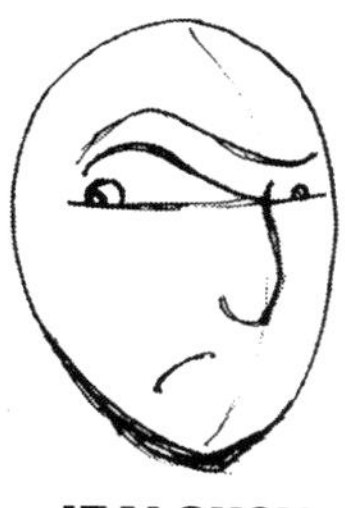

JEALOUSY

My Self-Esteem

Many people who experience jealousy do so to alleviate their feelings of low self-esteem, often unconsciously. Your self-esteem may be better than you think. Review your self-esteem by completing the sentence fragments:

I could have a positive attitude if ______________________________

____

I would value myself more if ______________________________

____

Others would value me more if I ______________________________

____

I am competent at ______________________________

____

I am threatened by others' successes because I ______________________________

____

Of Whom Am I Jealous?

In the table that follows, identify people you are jealous of. In the second column indicate why you feel jealous. In the third column, list why these jealousies might be unwarranted.

Of Whom I Am Jealous	Why I Feel Jealous	Why I Should Not be Jealous

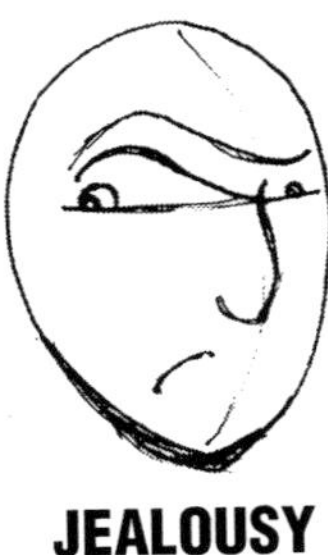

Comparisons

You can overcome jealousy by avoiding comparisons. In the table that follows, identify those people to whom you compare yourself and why you do so.

To Whom Do I Compare Myself?	Why Do I Compare Myself?

What I Have (and Want)

Concentrate on what you have rather than what other people have. Often we have more than we realize. For the following activity, identify all that you have (people, traits, things, etc.) and what you want:

I have ...

____

____

____

____

____

I want ...

____

____

____

____

____

Forgive Yourself

Write a letter forgiving yourself for a situation about which you feel guilty. If you can write about more than one situation, copy this form and complete it also.

I feel guilty about ______________________________

I wish that I had not done it, or had done it differently. I accept my actions. I am aware of my responsibility in the matter and I am ready to move on and do better in the future. I will work very hard to not do it again.

______________________________ NAME

______________ DATE

Nurture Yourself

By taking a 'time-out,' you can reduce anxiety through small acts of kindness toward yourself on a daily basis. Allow yourself to make time each day to nurture yourself, to step away from your duties at work and home. When you nurture yourself you begin to develop a loving relationship with YOU!

Some of the nurturing activities you can do for and by yourself are listed below. Place a check in the box in front of those you already do or plan to do and then use the blank lines to extend the list of activities you might try.

- ❑ Take a walk
- ❑ Take a long bubble bath
- ❑ Go to a matinee movie alone
- ❑ Meditate
- ❑ Watch a sunset
- ❑ Watch children play
- ❑ Plant a garden
- ❑ Listen to your favorite music
- ❑ Play with a pet
- ❑ Do yoga
- ❑ Read a mystery novel
- ❑ Drink a cup of tea
- ❑ Take a class
- ❑ ____________________
- ❑ ____________________
- ❑ ____________________
- ❑ ____________________
- ❑ ____________________
- ❑ ____________________
- ❑ Get a massage
- ❑ Read an inspirational book
- ❑ Work on a crossword puzzle
- ❑ Write in a journal
- ❑ Watch people at a local park
- ❑ "Smell the roses"
- ❑ Rent and watch videos
- ❑ Browse in a bookstore
- ❑ Ride a horse
- ❑ Visit a museum
- ❑ Learn a foreign language
- ❑ Play computer games
- ❑ Go outdoors and breathe deeply
- ❑ ____________________
- ❑ ____________________
- ❑ ____________________
- ❑ ____________________
- ❑ ____________________
- ❑ ____________________

Coping with Emotional Pain

Table of Contents and Facilitator Notes

Example:

People I Blame	Why I Blame This Person	How I Can Take Responsibility
My brother	*He was the baby in the family and got more attention than I did.*	*I teased him constantly. I didn't understand that it wasn't his fault.*

After participants have completed the handout, ask for volunteers to share one of the negative emotions they are feeling. Ask if anyone else in the group feels the same way. Often, knowing that others share similar feelings can be comforting.

Brainstorm possible situations that one might have that would cause emotional pain. (Betrayal, an argument, loss of a loved one, a huge disappointment.) Then distribute handouts.

Most people love music. Ask participants to think of songs that reflect emotional pain. They can name the piece of music, recite the words or sing it. Then distribute handouts.

Example:

Emotional Pain	How I Am Stronger
Sadness	*EX: I lost my loved one and thought I would never be able to survive. I found out that I am much more self-sufficient than I ever believed.*

After handouts are completed, ask for a volunteer to come up to the board and draw a picture that shows the volunteer having fun. Ask for participants to guess the action drawn.

Table of Contents and Facilitator Notes

Example:

Emotional Pain	Who	What the Person Does	How I Can Overcome My Feelings
Jealousy	*Neighbor*	*Brags all the time*	*I need to remember that I don't need to brag and it's too bad that he does!*

After completing the handout, ask participants to choose their number one Feel Good item. Then ask volunteers to share.

Prior to distributing the handouts, ask participants to define empathy.

Example:

People	Aspects of My Life	Other
My mom	*I have a good job*	*I love the sunshine*

Prior to participants completing handout, explain that writing this letter will help express their feelings about what has happened to cause emotional pain. Explain that they do not need to send the letter. The simple expression of their feelings will be helpful and possibly lead to deeper understanding of their feelings and solutions.

After handouts are completed, ask for one volunteer to write on the board. Ask participants to call out the activities that help them forget their troubles. Note how many repeats and how many new ideas are shared.

After handouts are completed, ask for volunteers to share their responses to "Write about a time when you were injured and hurt emotionally by your own attitude." Ask if they learned something from their own examples and from the examples of others.

Prior to distributing handouts, ask volunteers to describe a situation or event in which they received help from others.

After completing handouts, read through the list and ask for a show of hands from the participants who have felt these symptoms and believed the symptoms might have been from a stressful, emotional situation. Note the commonality of many of the symptoms.

Coping with Emotional Pain Introduction and Directions

Name____ Date________________

Everyone at some time experience some type of emotional pain. However, for some people these feelings are more intense and have the power to do more damage than others. Emotional pain can become so intense that it diminishes your life satisfaction. The *Coping with Emotional Pain Scale* can help you identify and explore the intensity of your feelings of emotional pain.

The assessment contains 30 statements. With TRUE or FALSE as your choice, read each of the statements and circle which best describes whether the statement applies to you or not.

When coping with emotional pain . . .	**TRUE**	**FALSE**
I often pretend I don't feel it	(1)	2

In the above statement, the circled 1 means that the statement is TRUE for the person completing the scale.

This is not a test. Since there are no right or wrong answers, do not spend too much time thinking about your answers. Your initial response will be the most true for you. Be sure to respond to every statement.

Turn to the next page and begin.

Coping with Emotional Pain Scale

When coping with emotional pain . . .	TRUE	FALSE
I often pretend I don't feel it	1	2
I work to process my emotions	2	1
I will allow myself time to heal properly	2	1
I don't want to address it	1	2
I engage in activities that will take my mind off the pain	2	1
I don't understand the feelings I have	1	2
I talk about my feelings with a trusted friend	2	1
I confront my irrational thoughts	2	1
I let others convince me my feelings aren't real	1	2
I blame myself	1	2
I try to find the life lesson in my pain	2	1
I remember what I have to be thankful for	2	1
I take my pain out on others	1	2
I let others pressure me into "getting over it"	1	2
I try not to dwell on my emotions	2	1
I blame others	1	2
I have processed the pain and moved through it	2	1
I allow my pain to define who I am	1	2
I allow myself sufficient "me time"	2	1
I avoid dealing with my feelings	1	2
I write about my feelings in a journal or diary	2	1
I express my feelings in healthy ways	2	1
I see crying as a sign of weakness and don't do it	1	2
I try not to vent my feelings on others around me	2	1
I engage in destructive behavior to forget	1	2
I engage in creative activities	2	1
I accept that it is normal to feel emotional pain	2	1
I often wonder if the emotional pain will ever subside	1	2
I abuse substances to forget about the feelings	1	2
I will seek professional help if I need it	2	1

Total number of answers circled = ______________

Go to the Scoring Directions on the next page

Coping with Emotional Pain Scale Scoring Directions

It is critical to begin to learn about and understand the effect that emotional pain is having on you, your relationships and career. The *Coping with Emotional Pain Scale* is designed to measure the level of intensity that your emotional interferes with your daily functioning.

For each of the items you completed on the previous page, add the numbers that you circled. Put that total on the line marked TOTAL at the end of the page.

Then, transfer your total to the space below.

Emotional Pain TOTAL = ___________

Profile Interpretation

Scale Score	Result	Indications
30 - 39	low	If you scored in the low range on the scale, you are not coping well with your emotional pain.
40 - 50	moderate	If you scored in the moderate range on the scale, you are coping fairly well with your emotional pain.
51 - 60	high	If you scored in the high range on the scale, you are coping well with your emotional pain.

No matter how you scored, low, moderate or high, you will benefit from these exercises that follow.

The Blame Game

Do you blame anyone for your emotional pain? Playing this blame-game can actually increase your pain rather than reducing it. NOW is the time to stop playing the blame game. Below, identify the people you blame for your emotional pain, why you blame them and then let go of this blame by taking responsibility for your actions.

People I Blame	Why I Blame This Person	How I Can Take Responsibility

What Am I Feeling?

In the space below, write or draw all of the negative feelings you are feeling right now.

My Emotional Pain Worksheet

It is important to explore the reasons you are experiencing emotional pain. Examples are a recent divorce, abuse as a child or partner, or death of a loved one. Below is a process for effectively facing and accepting your emotional pain.

Step 1: What is a recent situation that prompted your emotional pain? ____________________

____

____

Step 2: Acknowledge your feelings. I feel ____________________

____

____

Step 3: Accept what happened. This is what happened ____________________

____

____

Step 4: Feel it. I will allow myself to feel it by ____________________

____

____

Step 5: Don't mask it. In the past, I have masked the feeling by____________________

____

____

Step 6: Learn from it. I have learned the following from my emotional pain: ____________________

____

____

Step 7: Work through your feelings. I will work through my feelings to overcome my emotional pain by____________________

____

____

Emotional Pain Music

Creativity can help to free you from your emotional pain. Below, write a song that describes what you're feeling and going through. You may want to change the words to a tune you already know.

TITLE

I Am Stronger!

Often, emotional pain can make you stronger. What are some of the unexpected strengths you have discovered in yourself – learned as a result of your emotional pain? Below, identify your emotional pain and how it has made you stronger.

The situation prompting my emotional pain is ______________________________

____

____

Emotional Pain	How I Am Stronger
Sadness	
Jealousy	
Anger	
Loneliness	
Anxiety & Worry	
Other	
Other	

Choose a Light, Fun Activity!

It is difficult to feel sad or anxious if you are watching a movie, playing a game of chess, riding a roller coaster, listening to your favorite music or playing with a pet. Choose to have fun and permit yourself to take a break from your emotional pain. In what ways could you have fun?

Describe or draw what you can do to take your mind off of your emotional pain.

By Yourself	With Family
With Friends	In Community (volunteering, spiritual pursuits, etc.)

Who Provokes Me?

Identify the people whom you allow to provoke you and what they do to provoke you, thereby causing you emotional pain. Consider how you can overcome these feelings.

Emotional Pain	Who	What This Person Does	How I Can Overcome My Feelings
Jealousy			
Anger			
Worry & Anxiety			
Loneliness			
Sadness			

I Feel Good About Me!

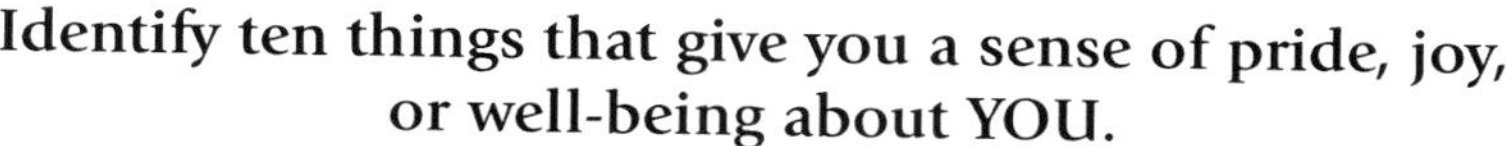

Identify ten things that give you a sense of pride, joy, or well-being about YOU.

1. ____

2. ____

3. ____

4. ____

5. ____

6. ____

7. ____

8. ____

9. ____

10. ____

Empathetic People

There will be times when you feel your emotional pain is too deep to say aloud or publicly. You might think that nobody could possibly understand what you are experiencing. The truth is that all people have experienced emotional pain and you need to find people who will be empathetic to your pain. **Empathy is the ability to put yourself in the position of other people, and vice versa.** Who are the people in your life who will empathically listen to you?

Complete the following chart and keep it available to remind you of people to contact when you need an empathetic person with whom you can talk.

Empathetic Person	What I Would Feel Comfortable Talking About

If you are not able to list several empathetic people who are in your life, it may be time to find a professional with whom to talk.

What I Am Thankful For

Sometimes in moments of pain, we forget what we have to be thankful for. Being thankful for what you have, for even the most basic things, events and people, can help you overcome trauma and find balance in your life. Below, people, aspects of your life, and the other things for which you are thankful.

People	Aspects of My Life	Other

My Letter

Write a letter to someone in your past (or present)who has caused (or is causing) you pain.

Dear ________________________________:
(NAME OF PERSON)

I am writing to let you know how I feel about what happened between us . . .

____

____

____

____

I feel . . .

____

____

____

____

____

____

____

____

____

____

____

____
NAME

This letter was designed to help you express your feelings about what has happened to cause you emotional pain. Sign the letter, but do not feel like you need to send the letter. The simple expression of your feelings will be helpful.

Get Your Mind Off YOU!

It's time to move on from your emotional pain. You can distract your thinking by forgetting it for a while. You may not be ready or able to forget about it and move on, but you will give yourself a break. Think about some recreation activities that bring you pleasure. These activities can be done alone or with other people.

What activities do you enjoy that bring you a sense of relaxation?

What activities do you enjoy so much that you can forget your own troubles?

What are your favorite hobbies and leisure activities?

What activities do you feel passionate about? What activities bring you meaning and a sense of purpose?

What can you do to have some good laughs?

Emotional Pain Quote

> *"We are injured and hurt emotionally, not so much by other people or what they say and don't say, but by our own attitude and our own response."*
>
> ~ **Maxwell Maltz**

Write about a time when you were injured and hurt emotionally by other people?

____

____

Write about a time when you were injured and hurt emotionally by someone.

____

____

Write about a time when you were injured and hurt emotionally by what someone didn't say to you, but said to someone else.

____

____

Write about a time when you were injured and hurt emotionally by your own attitude.

____

____

Write about a time when you were injured and hurt emotionally by your own response.

____

____

Refocus

You can overcome your emotional pain by refocusing on others who also have problems. It is difficult to completely focus on two things at the same time. Take a break from your own pain by helping other people. This type of giving can help to heal your spirit. In the spaces that follow, identify ways you can help others.

Others I Can Help	How I Can Help Them

Emotional Pain Can Cause Physical Pain

Emotional pain can create or aggravate the physical pain you are experiencing. People may say it's all in your head, but often you experience it in your body too. All systems of the body can be affected by physical problems and they can also be affected by emotional stress.

Check off the symptoms that you experience from time to time:

- ❑ Abnormal stomach activity
- ❑ Back pain
- ❑ Butterflies in the stomach
- ❑ Chest feels heavy
- ❑ Chest pains
- ❑ Cold
- ❑ Cold feet
- ❑ Cold hands
- ❑ Cramps
- ❑ Depression
- ❑ Dizziness
- ❑ Eating disorders
- ❑ Fatigue
- ❑ Flu
- ❑ Headache
- ❑ Heart aches
- ❑ Heartburn
- ❑ High blood pressure
- ❑ Inability to breathe easily
- ❑ Increased heart rate
- ❑ Infections
- ❑ Jaw pain
- ❑ Muscle tension
- ❑ Muscle tightness
- ❑ Neck pain
- ❑ Reproductive problems
- ❑ Runny nose
- ❑ Shortness of breath
- ❑ Shoulder pain
- ❑ Skin problems
- ❑ Sleep disturbances
- ❑ Sweaty palms or hands
- ❑ Tired eyes
- ❑ Other ______________________

When do these symptoms occur?

____

____

____

Describe the frequency of these symptoms when you are stressed out? Explain what you have noticed that worsens them and what relieves them.

____

____

____

Level of Physical Pain

Table of Contents and Facilitator Notes

Ask participants to silently read the meditation script a few times. Then ask them to try the meditation.

Prior to participants reading the italicized copy to themselves, go around the room with each person reading one indented line.

After practicing in class, suggest that participants take the handout home and practice there. Perhaps they can share their results at the next session.

After completing the handout, ask participants to share the various ways they work to maintain a stress-free mindset.

Prior to completing the handout, ask participants to answer the question, "What are some negative ways of dealing with pain?" Write their responses on the board.

After handout is completed, ask participants to call out their favorite physical exercise and sports and write them on a board, suggesting they write good ideas that they are willing to consider on the back of their handout.

Ask participants to describe their favorite activities that act as distractions from their pain. Ask "Why is the activity effective in distracting you?"

Table of Contents and Facilitator Notes

Ask participants, "What is the definition of a lifestyle?" After people have responded, discuss how lifestyle choices can affect the kinds and levels of pain experienced. Ask people to talk about their positive and negative lifestyle choices and how these choices affect their personal pain.

Example:

Substances	Quantity I Consume Each Day	How I Can Make a Positive Lifestyle Change
Caffeine	*Five Cups of coffee a day and two sodas*	*Drink a cup of coffee in the a.m. and one in the p.m., and substitute lemonade for soda.*

Ask participants to talk about their experiences in various support groups.

Tell participants to draw how they feel when they are in pain. Explain that they will not be judged on their creative abilities. Have participants share their illustrations.

Before beginning the session, ask for a few volunteers (who like to doodle) to come up to the board or flip chart and doodle themselves doodling on the board or flip chart.

After they have read the visualization, ask participants to practice the visualization. Ask them to talk about how it made them feel.

Prior to distributing the handout, discuss the concept of exercise and how it can work to help reduce various types of pain.

Explain to participants that developing a workout schedule can help to keep them motivated.

Example:

Type of Exercise	How Many Times a Week?	How Much Time Spent?
Walk briskly	*4-5*	*45 minutes each day*

Level of Physical Pain Scale Introduction and Directions

Name ____ **Date** ______________

Physical pain is any body pain signaling something wrong in the body that needs to be fixed. There are many different ways of coping with physical pain, often determined by the level of pain you are experiencing. An inability to cope with pain can affect all aspects of your life. Medication is one way of coping with pain, but there are also non-medication based ways of coping to consider.

The purpose of this assessment is to help you identify the level of physical pain you are currently experiencing. For both of the sections that follow, read each of the statements and decide if the statement applies to you always, sometimes or never. If it is always true for you, circle the number 3 next to the statement. If it is sometimes true for you, circle the number 2 next to the statement. If it is never true for you, circle the number 1, next to the statement. Complete all of the items before going back to score this scale.

In the following example, the circled 1 indicates that the item is never true for the participant completing the assessment:

	Always	Sometimes	Never
Because of the pain I have . . .			
I have a difficult time getting out of bed	3	2	(1)

This is not a test. Since there are no right or wrong answers, do not spend too much time thinking about your answers. Your initial response will be the most true for you.
Be sure to respond to every statement.

Turn to the next page and begin.

Level of Physical Pain Scale

Because of the pain I have . . .	Always	Sometimes	Never
I have a difficult time getting out of bed	3	2	1
I can't work eight hours a day	3	2	1
I can't perform basic household chores	3	2	1
I feel hopeless about my life	3	2	1
I can't make plans for the weekends	3	2	1
I can't do chores outside the house	3	2	1
I feel discouraged	3	2	1
I can't volunteer in the community	3	2	1
I can't engage in my favorite leisure activities	3	2	1
I have no social life	3	2	1

A - TOTAL = ____________

Continued on the next page

Level of Physical Pain Scale *Continued*

Because of the pain I have . . .	Always	Sometimes	Never
I feel exhausted after a full night of sleep	3	2	1
I can't enjoy life	3	2	1
I can't focus or concentrate	3	2	1
I get frustrated	3	2	1
I can't deal with the side effects of my medications	3	2	1
I am not available for anyone who needs me	3	2	1
I can't hang out with my friends	3	2	1
I can't exercise like I want	3	2	1
I can't get enough sleep	3	2	1
I have sudden mood changes	3	2	1

B - TOTAL = ____________

Go to the Scoring Directions on the next page

Level of Physical Pain Scale

The *Level of Physical Pain Scale* is designed to help you learn how your pain is affecting your life.

Scoring Directions

Look at the items you just completed.

Add the numbers you've circled for each of the two sections (A and B) on the previous pages.

Put that total on the line marked TOTAL at the end of each section.

Transfer your totals for each of the two sections to the lines below:

A Total = ___________

B Total = ___________

Level of Physical Pain Total = ___________

The Profile Interpretation section below will help you understand your scores.

Profile Interpretation

Scale Score	Result	Indications
20 to 33	low	If you scored in the low range on any of the scales, you are probably not experiencing much pain in your life.
34 to 46	moderate	If you scored in the moderate range on any of the scales, you are probably experiencing some pain in your life.
47 to 60	high	If you scored in the high range on any of the scales, you are probably experiencing a great deal of pain in your life.

Meditation

One of the best ways to cope with pain is meditation, a special thinking process. Many types of meditations exist. The *Breath Counting Meditation* can be very effective for pain management. Try the following meditation to help promote pain relief and peace.

Be seated.
Find a relaxing posture.
Keep your back straight, but try to center yourself.
Take several deep breaths.
Close your eyes or fix them on a spot about three feet in front of you.

As you continue to breathe, focus your attention on each part of your breaths.
Concentrate on your breath as you inhale; then, as you exhale, count "one."
Concentrate on your next breath; then as you exhale, count "two."
Concentrate on your next breath; then as you exhale, count "three."
Continue the count until you reach ten; then begin over again with one.
If you lose count, simply start over with one.

Try to block out all thoughts that seem to be streaming through your mind.
When you discover that your mind begins to focus on a thought,
refocus your attention on counting your breaths.
Simply let the thoughts slip away and return your attention to your next breath
and begin the counting process again.

As you find your mind fixating on your pain,
acknowledge the pain and return to counting your breaths.
Try to focus your attention on the sensations of breathing and away from your pain.

After you have read the process, try this meditation for several minutes.

How did you feel?

____

____

How did it affect your pain?

____

____

Total-Body Relaxation

Pain manifests itself through physical symptoms in your body. Total Body Relaxation (often called Progressive Muscle Relaxation) is a simple technique used to stop pain by relaxing all of the muscles throughout your body, one group at a time. Read through the following script several timesbefore you attempt to do Total Body Relaxation.

Take a few deep breaths, and begin to relax.
Get comfortable and put aside all of your worries.
Let each part of your body begin to relax… starting with your feet.
Imagine your feet relaxing as all of your tension begins to fade away.
Imagine the relaxation moving up into your calves and thighs … feel them beginning to relax.
Continue now to let the relaxation move into your hips and stomach.
Allow the relaxation to move into your waist.
Your entire body from the waist down is now completely relaxed.
Let go of any strain and discomfort you might feel.
Allow the relaxation to move into your chest until your chest feels completely relaxed.
Just enjoy the feeling of complete relaxation.
Continue to let the relaxation move through the muscles of your shoulders, then spread down into your upper arms, into your elbows, and finally all the way down to your wrists and hands.
Put aside all of your worries.
Let yourself be totally present in the moment and let yourself relax more and more.
Let all the muscles in your neck unwind and let the relaxation move into your chin and jaws.
Feel the tension around your eyes flow away as the relaxation moves throughout your face and head.
Feel your forehead relax and your entire head beginning to feel lighter.
Let yourself drift deeper and deeper into relaxation and peace.

After you have read the above paragraph several times, find a quiet location where you can practice Total Body Relaxation. Assume a comfortable position in a chair. Take off your jewelry/glasses so that you are totally free. Try to let the relaxation happen without having to force it. If during the relaxation you lose concentration, don't be concerned, begin again.

How did you feel?

____

____

How did it affect your pain?

____

____

Learning to Breathe Deeply

Deep breathing can help relax your body and ease your pain. Tight muscles and muscle tension can be drastically diminished by breathing properly. Practice the deep breathing exercise below to see if you can reduce the pain in your body. Prior to practicing this exercise, find a quiet location and block out distracting thoughts. Imagine a spot directly below your navel and concentrate on it as you do the exercise. As you get better at breathing deeply, you will be able to use deep breathing to calm the pain you are experiencing.

Abdominal Breathing

When you are relaxed, you breathe fully and deeply, from your abdomen. It is virtually impossible to be tense and breathe from your abdomen. Abdominal breathing triggers a relaxation response in you.

Shallow, Chest-Level Breathing

When you are tense, your breathing usually becomes shallow and rapid, occurring high in your chest. With this type of breathing you tend to over-breathe and hyperventilate. If you breathe like this in certain situations, it's okay. You can retrain yourself to breathe deeply from your abdomen. Try this now:

Abdominal Breathing Exercise

Inhale slowly through your nose, down deep as possible into your lungs. You should see your abdomen rise. When you have taken a full breath, pause for a moment and then exhale slowly through your nose or mouth. Be sure to exhale thoroughly.

Take ten of these full abdominal breaths. Keep your breaths as smooth and regular as possible. As you continue this process, you can try slowing down the rate at which you take breaths. Pause for a second after each breath you take.

On a scale from 1 (a little) to 10 (a lot), how does deep breathing reduce your feelings of pain?

____

____

____

____

____

____

Maintain a Healthy Stress-Free Mindset

The suggestions below can assist you in maintaining a healthy stress-free and pain-free mind set:

Check the items that you presently do:

- ❑ Accept and set aside what cannot be controlled
- ❑ Assert yourself in positive ways
- ❑ Avoid hot-button topics
- ❑ Be able to say No
- ❑ Be aware and accept that unexpected problems will arise
- ❑ Believe that you will succeed if you keep working toward your goals
- ❑ Breathe deeply
- ❑ Compromise willingly
- ❑ Eat nutritionally
- ❑ Engage in yoga
- ❑ Enjoy life's simple pleasures
- ❑ Express your feelings
- ❑ Focus on the positive
- ❑ Have a support system and ask for their help
- ❑ Journal about your feelings associated with stress
- ❑ Know that there are some things you cannot control
- ❑ Learn to forgive
- ❑ Look at the big picture
- ❑ Manage your time
- ❑ Meditate or pray
- ❑ Participate in activities for fun
- ❑ Plan your time effectively
- ❑ Realize that setbacks are temporary
- ❑ Reduce your to-do list
- ❑ Relax with calming music
- ❑ Take control of your environment
- ❑ Think positively in challenging situations
- ❑ Try to avoid people who stress you out

Now – highlight the above strategies you are going to incorporate in your life.

Unhealthy Ways of Coping with Pain

Check the items that describe the unhealthy ways you cope with your pain:

- ❑ Allowing yourself to be a workaholic
- ❑ Constant napping
- ❑ Crying continually
- ❑ Discontinuing the enjoyable activities you are still physically able to do
- ❑ Emailing, texting and/or telephoning in excess
- ❑ Engaging continually with social media
- ❑ Engaging exclusively with social media
- ❑ Mis-managing food leading to an eating disorder
- ❑ Over-eating
- ❑ Over-medicating
- ❑ Refusing to admit that something may be wrong (Denial)
- ❑ Resisting therapy or other valid recommendations
- ❑ Sitting for hours in front of the TV, computer, electronic games
- ❑ Sleeping too little
- ❑ Sleeping too much
- ❑ Unwilling to talk with someone about the pain
- ❑ Using alcoholic drinks in excess to relax
- ❑ Using drugs
- ❑ Withdrawing from friends and family
- ❑ Yelling, angry outbursts, bullying
- ❑ Other______________________________
- ❑ Other______________________________
- ❑ Other______________________________
- ❑ Other______________________________

Sign below. Make a commitment to begin the process of discontinuing the unhealthy ways you cope with pain that you checked above.

____________________________________ ________________________

SIGNATURE DATE

Reducing Pain with Everyday Exercise

You have many choices of ways to reduce pain before it spirals into a heightened, debilitating state. Involve yourself with distractions that allow you to focus on things outside of yourself. Physical exercise is one of the most powerful tools for reducing anxiety because it directly impacts the physiological and psychological factors that underlie anxiety.

What are your favorite exercises and how often do you participate in them?

____

____

MY PLAN to exercise more:

____

____

What sports do you like to play and how often do you participate in them?

____

____

MY PLAN to participate in more sports:

____

____

Which household chores provide exercise and how often do you participate in them?

____

____

MY PLAN to participate in more active household chores:

____

____

What are some things you do, or could do in your community to get exercise?

____

____

MY PLAN to participate in more community activities:

____

____

Distraction

When you focus on your pain, it actually makes things worse than better. Instead, try to find things that you enjoy doing. By engaging in activities that keep you from thinking about your pain, you might not be able to avoid the pain, but you can avoid focusing on it and begin to regain control over your life.

Activities I Can Do that I Enjoy and that Can Distract Me

Lifestyle Choices

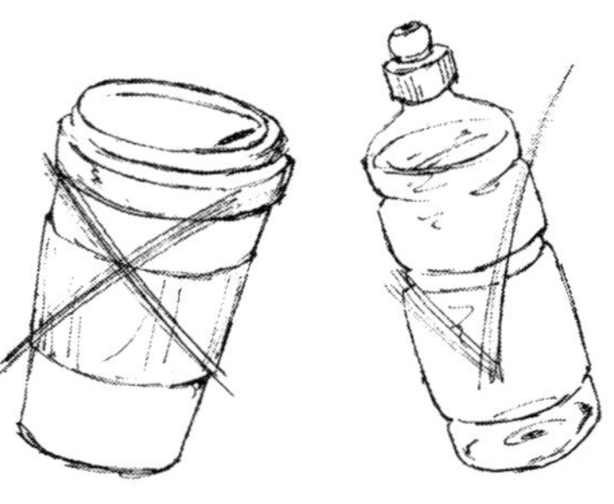

Lifestyle choices are responsible for a large number of health issues and pain. Positive changes can greatly reduce the amount of pain you are experiencing. Several lifestyle changes can make your life healthier and less painful. Let's examine some possible changes:

Substances	Quantity I Consume Each Day	How I Can Make a Positive Lifestyle Change
Caffeine		
Alcoholic beverages		
Nicotine		
Sugar or Artificial Sweeteners		
Soda		
Red, Fatty Meats		
Other unhealthy/junk foods __________ __________ __________ __________ __________ __________ __________ __________ __________ __________		

Support Groups

When people are with others who experience the similar types of emotional and/or physical pain, they tend to feel less isolated and supported. They are able to share ideas, tips and suggestions about pain management, resources, vital information learned through research and experience – and just as important – share feelings and coping methods.

How does (or can) a support group help you to …

… feel that you are not alone? ____________________

____

… feel like you are part of a community? ____________________

____

… tell your story about the pain? ____________________

____

… take a more realistic view? ____________________

____

… share coping resources? ____________________

____

… empower yourself? ____________________

____

… feel supported? ____________________

____

… trust others and be trusted? ____________________

____

Where is the closest applicable support group to you? ____________________

____

If there isn't a support group close to you, consider starting one. Gather friends with like-minded issues and share.

Illustrating My Pain

Draw a picture of yourself when you are feeling pain. Try to show what you feel.

Doodling or Writing about Pain

Doodling is an excellent way for you to unleash the power of self-expression. You do not need to be an artist to doodle. You are the only one who needs to know what the doodle represents. Doodling is simply drawing something without thinking a lot about it. It is designed to help you put your left-brain (your logical brain) on hold while you use your right-brain (the creative part of your brain). Doodles can be silly designs, drawings, abstract shapes, or simply lines.

Pain makes me feel like . . .	**Pain forces me to miss out on . . .**
What I will start doing to lessen my pain . . .	**What my life would be like without pain . . .**

Visualization - Using Mental Imagery

Working with images can be a useful way to reduce anxiety. Mental Imagery is the use of memories of visual events and experiences to project a mental image in your mind. Notice that vision, hearing, sense of smell and physical sensations of warmth and sand are included.

Imagine that you are resting on a white, sandy beach.

The water is turquoise and the sky is clear and blue.

You can hear the soft waves of the ocean as the tide gently rolls in and splashes in and then goes out again.

Imagine looking out over the water toward the horizon.

Look up at the sky, noticing a few white, fluffy clouds.

You feel relaxed and calm.

You can feel the warmth of the sand on your feet.

Notice the warmth of the sun on your face and shoulders.

Imagine picking up some soft sand and letting it sift through your fingers.

Now imagine lying on a blanket and closing your eyes.

Notice the sounds that you hear – the playful call of seagulls, the waves rolling in and out, and other people walking on the beach.

Take a deep breath and smell the clean, fresh ocean air.

Simply enjoy lying on the beach for several minutes.

Now, write out a pleasant imagery scene, one that you will like picturing and remembering. Use as many senses as possible. When you find yourself in an anxiety-producing situation, you can begin to imagine this scene vividly.

____

____

____

____

____

____

____

____

____

____

Cardiovascular Exercises

Physical inactivity can increase the pain you experience. Cardiovascular exercise comes in many different forms for different people. Check with your physician regarding the level of activity appropriate for you. Activities that have been found to be especially beneficial when performed regularly:

- Brisk walking, hiking, climbing stairs instead of taking the elevator, doing aerobic exercises in your home or a gym, doing calisthenics
- Jogging, running, and bicycling
- Swimming, rowing, and water aerobics
- Sports including tennis, golf, racquetball, soccer, basketball, softball
- Walking your pet, gardening, and working in the yard and around the house
- Dancing

List the ways you exercise aerobically and how often you do them each week:

✓ ____
✓ ____
✓ ____
✓ ____
✓ ____
✓ ____
✓ ____
✓ ____
✓ ____
✓ ____

List the excuses you give for not exercising aerobically:

✓ ____
✓ ____
✓ ____
✓ ____
✓ ____
✓ ____
✓ ____
✓ ____
✓ ____
✓ ____

Your Workout Schedule

It is important to develop your own workout schedule to provide you with maximum benefit from aerobic exercise. Some people tend to exercise in the mornings, while others prefer the evenings.

List your current workout schedule in the spaces below.

My CURRENT Workout Schedule

Type of Exercise	How Many Times a Week?	How Much Time Spent?

My IDEAL Workout Schedule

Type of Exercise	How Many Times a Week?	How Much Time Spent?

Pain Management

Table of Contents and Facilitator Notes

Table of Contents and Facilitator Notes

Example:

Day	Time	Rate Your Amount of Pain (Least) 1	2	3	4	(Most) 5	What are You Usually Doing at that Time?
Monday	*Morning*	✓					*Breakfast, go to work*
	Afternoon		✓				*Work*
	Evening			✓			*Home, make dinner, clean up*
	Night					✓	*Try to sleep, can't get comfortable*

Suggest that participants keep this log updated at all times and make several photocopies for doctors and family.

Go around the group and have participants take turns reading each of the sentence fragments and suggest how they would complete the sentence.

Before distributing the handout, ask the group "What are some positive ways of dealing with pain?" and "What are some negative ways of dealing with pain?"

After the group has completed the activity, ask for volunteers to read a sentence with their completion.

Suggest to participants who related to this quotation that they cut it out and post it in a place where they will see it often.

Discuss this page a day prior to implementing it. Ask participants to bring photographs as well as any magazine pictures, poetry or quotations they might have at home. In case they don't bring enough, have some magazines, quotations, etc., available. If you have poster board or larger sheets of paper available for everyone, use that instead of this. Ask them to write, My Pain-Free Journal on the top.

Pain Management Scale
Introduction and Directions

Name ____ Date ________________

At times, managing your pain may be the best, or only, option available to you. When this is the case, understanding how much your pain is interfering with your normal daily functioning is the first step in effective pain management. The Pain Management Scale is designed to help you explore how your life is negatively affected by your daily pain.

For each of the items that follow, choose the response that best describes the effect pain is having on the various aspects of your life. In the following example, the circled numbers indicate how much the statement is descriptive of the person completing the inventory.

3 = Very Much **2 = A Little** **1 = Not At All**

I. My pain has interfered with...

1. My ability to do my job . . . . (3) 2 1
2. My ability to concentrate 3 2 (1)

This is not a test. Since there are no right or wrong answers, do not spend too much time thinking about your answers. Your initial response will be the most true for you. Be sure to respond to every statement.

Turn to the next page and begin.

Pain Management Scale

3 = Very Much 2 = A Little 1 = Not At All

I. My pain has interfered with . . .

1. My ability to do my job.	3	2	1
2. My ability to concentrate.	3	2	1
3. My ability to do my usual work.	3	2	1
4. My interest in my job.	3	2	1
5. My ability to keep a job.	3	2	1
6. My productivity at work.	3	2	1

TOTAL = ___________

II. My pain has interfered with . . .

7. How much I enjoy life.	3	2	1
8. My ability to take part in activities I enjoy.	3	2	1
9. My night's sleep..	3	2	1
10. My energy level.	3	2	1
11. My interest in sexual activity..	3	2	1
12. My desire to get going in the morning.	3	2	1

TOTAL = ___________

Continued on the next page

Pain Management Scale *Continued*

3 = Very Much **2 = A Little** **1 = Not At All**

III. My pain can be seen in . . .

13. My attitude.	3	2	1
14. My feelings of anxiety	3	2	1
15. The amount of frustration I experience.	3	2	1
16. The amount of anger I display.	3	2	1
17. My level of depression	3	2	1
18. My resentment	3	2	1

TOTAL = ___________

IV. My pain has affected . . .

19. My interest in meeting new people.	3	2	1
20. My ability to relate to others.	3	2	1
21. My relationship with my family.	3	2	1
22. My friendships	3	2	1
23. How others view me.	3	2	1
24. My time spent with other people	3	2	1

TOTAL = ___________

Go to the Scoring Directions on the next page

Pain Management Scale
Scoring Directions

The Pain Management Scale is designed to measure how pain is interfering with the way you usually live your life. For each of the sections, count the scores you circled for each of the four sections. Put that total on the line marked "Total" at the end of each section.

Then, transfer your totals to the spaces below:

TOTALS

I. ________ = **Work** (Your ability to function as usual on a job)

II. ________ = **Life Enjoyment** (Your contentment)

III. ________ = **Mood** (Your general feelings)

IV. ________ = **Relationships** (Your relations with other people)

Profile Interpretation

Individual Scale Score	Result	Indications
6 - 9	low	If you scored in the low range on any of the scales, it means that your pain is not interfering with your ability to live a normal life in these categories.
10 - 14	moderate	If you scored in the moderate range on any of the scales, it means that your pain is somewhat interfering with your ability to live a normal life in these categories.
15- 18	high	If you scored in the high range on any of the scales, it means that your pain is very much interfering with your ability to live a normal life in these categories.

My Pain Location

On the diagrams below, shade in the areas where you feel the most pain, or create your own color chart (one color for intense pain, moderate, slight, etc. Place an X where your pain hurts the most.

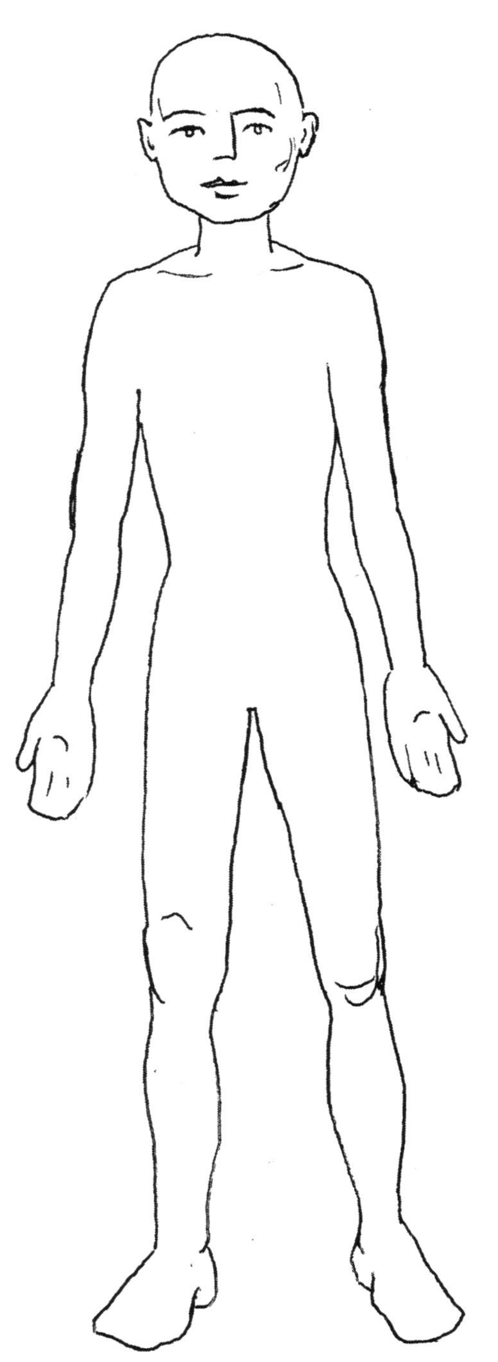

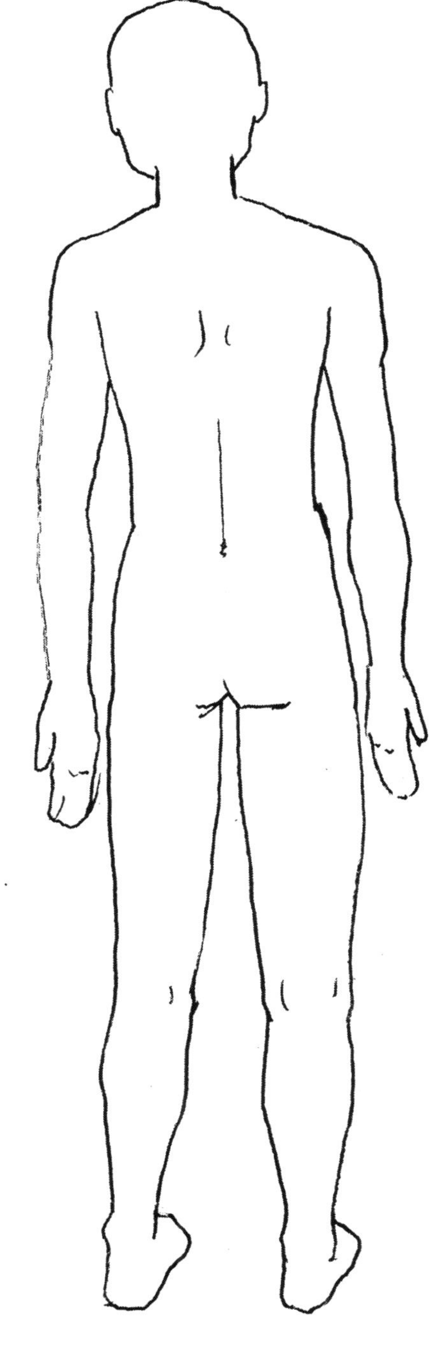

Describing My Pain WORD SEARCH

Many different words can describe the pain you feel. Circle the eight words that represent feelings that describe pain. Words may appear backwards, across, down, etc.

A	K	L	R	I	A	B	V	R	W	O	R	O	S
I	E	P	M	G	P	R	A	H	S	S	H	T	H
N	A	G	G	I	N	G	Y	T	L	O	A	Z	U
C	B	A	E	I	L	F	O	W	Q	B	D	S	O
F	G	U	R	T	T	H	R	O	B	B	I	N	G
L	N	A	R	G	I	N	G	I	F	M	L	W	O
A	I	T	O	N	N	T	N	F	D	J	U	G	A
W	H	P	S	H	I	G	Q	A	P	Y	E	I	S
E	C	X	E	S	T	N	E	D	L	I	P	J	E
D	G	N	A	W	I	N	G	P	E	F	J	O	D
X	C	T	S	H	O	O	T	I	N	G	I	N	G

Answers: throbbing, stabbing, shooting, burning, nagging, sharp, aching, gnawing

Pain Rating Scales

Complete the following rating scales to describe the amount of pain you are experiencing.

1) Circle the number that best describes your pain at its worst in the past 24 hours.

0 1 2 3 4 5 6 7 8 9 10

No Pain **Excruciating Pain**

2) Circle the number that best describes your pain at its least in the past 24 hours.

0 1 2 3 4 5 6 7 8 9 10

No Pain **Excruciating Pain**

3) Circle the number best describes your average amount of pain in the past 24 hours.

0 1 2 3 4 5 6 7 8 9 10

No Pain **Excruciating Pain**

4) Circle the number that best describes your level of pain right now.

0 1 2 3 4 5 6 7 8 9 10

No Pain **Excruciating Pain**

5) Circle the number that best describes how much relief are you receiving from pain treatments.

0 1 2 3 4 5 6 7 8 9 10

No Pain **Excruciating Pain**

6) Circle the number that best describes how much relief are you receiving from medications.

0 1 2 3 4 5 6 7 8 9 10

No Pain **Excruciating Pain**

My Pain History

Complete the following questions to begin to identify your pain history. If you need more space, turn the paper over and write on the back.

Where is your worst pain located?

____

When did your pain start?

____

What happened to cause your pain?

____

____

What makes it worse?

____

____

What does your pain feel like?

____

____

Is your pain constant, or does it come and go?

____

When do you experience pain (morning, afternoon, evening, night-time, all day?)

____

How long does your pain last?

____

What do you do to alleviate the pain?

____

____

How Pain Affects My Life

Pain can affect your health and well-being in many ways. In each of the spaces below, describe how pain has affected your life. If you need more space, continue writing on the back of this page.

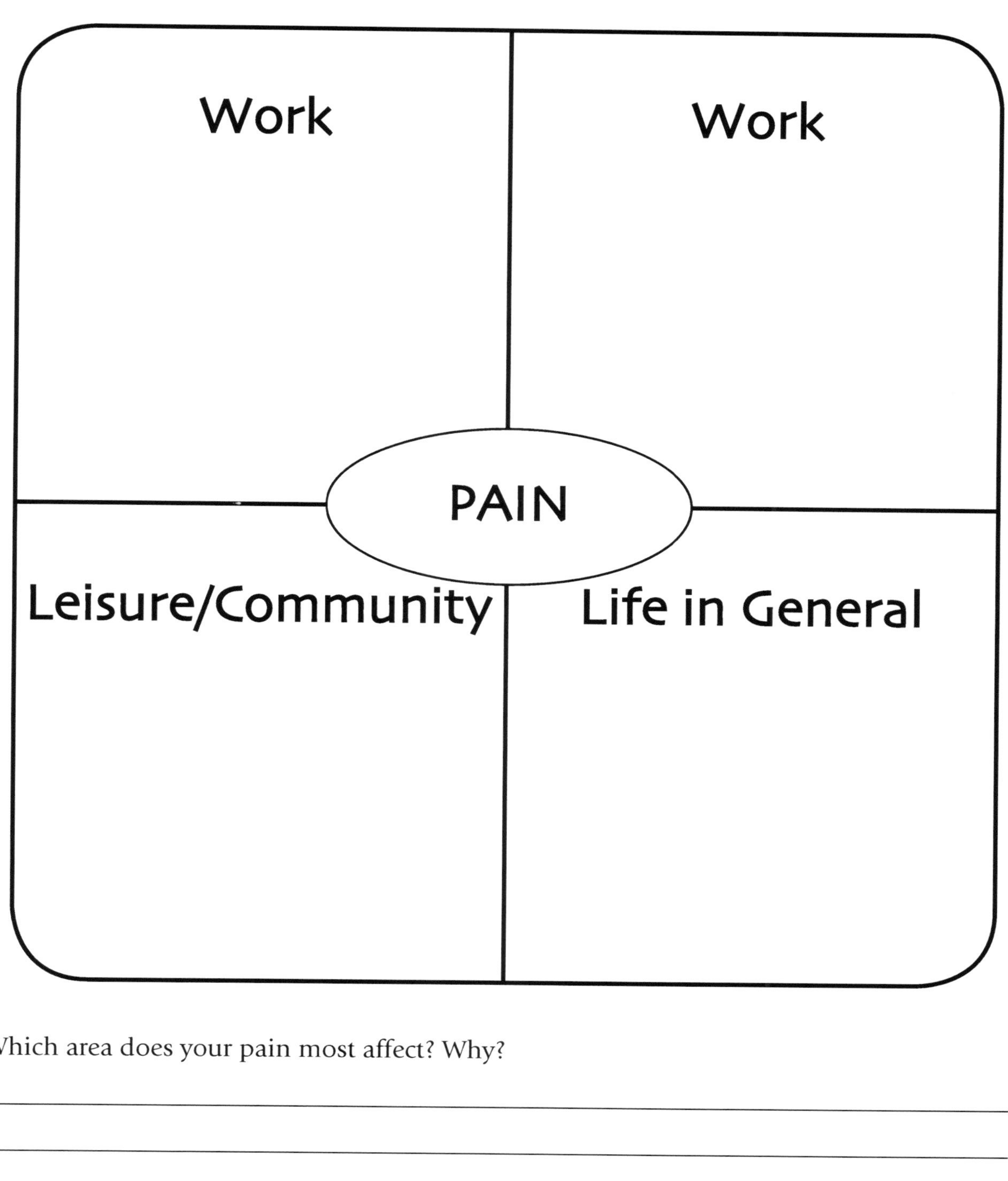

Which area does your pain most affect? Why?

____

____

____

Faces of Pain

Use the following assessment to describe how you feel today.
Place an X over the face that describes your pain on most days.

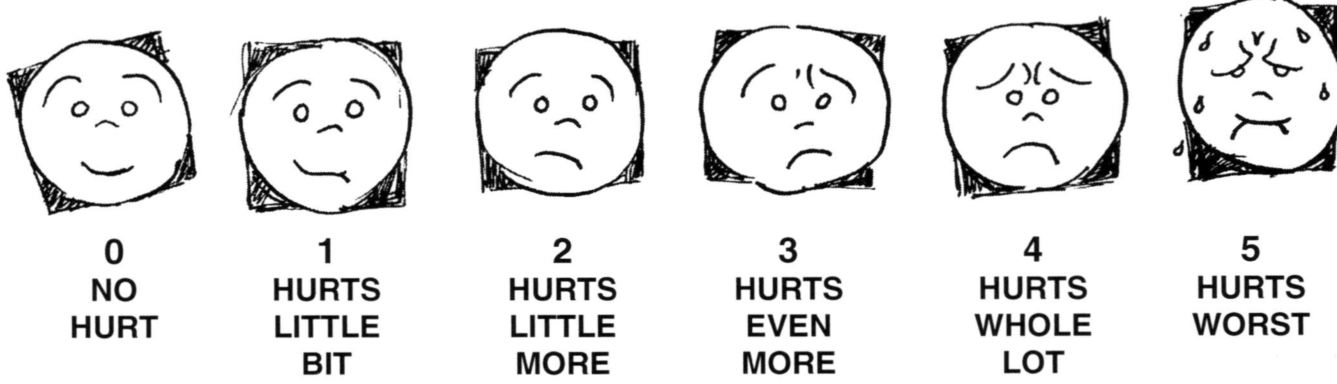

Now place an X over the face that describes the pain you would find acceptable.

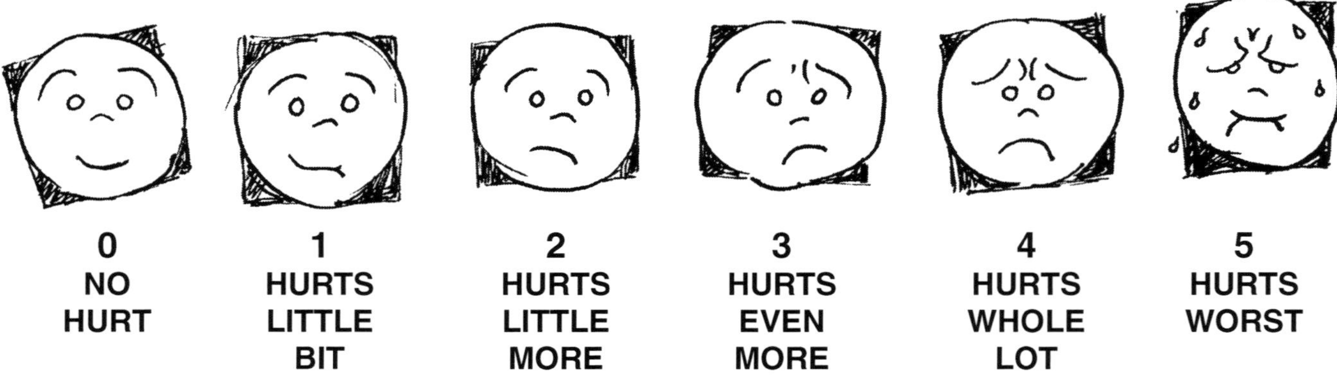

Pain Management Log

Use the chart that follows to help you manage your pain. Identify the types of medication you are taking, other pain control methods you've tried, and the activities you are engaged in when you feel pain.

Date & Time	Severity of Pain 0 = No Pain 10 = Severe Pain	Medicines Taken	Other Pain Control Methods Used	Activity at Time of Pain

Daily Pain Level

One particular pain is ______________________________

Identify your daily pain level every day for a week by placing an X in the blocks from 1 (Least Pain) to 5 (Most Pain).

Day	Time	Rate Your Amount of Pain (Least) 1	2	3	4	(Most) 5	What are You Usually Doing at That Time?
Monday	Morning						
	Afternoon						
	Evening						
	Night						
Tuesday	Morning						
	Afternoon						
	Evening						
	Night						
Wednesday	Morning						
	Afternoon						
	Evening						
	Night						
Thursday	Morning						
	Afternoon						
	Evening						
	Night						
Friday	Morning						
	Afternoon						
	Evening						
	Night						
Saturday	Morning						
	Afternoon						
	Evening						
	Night						
Sunday	Morning						
	Afternoon						
	Evening						
	Night						

Search for patterns related to when you feel the most pain, when you feel relatively pain-free and what you are doing at the time. What patterns do you see?

____

____

____

____

Pain Medication Log

You can use the following chart to manage the medicines you are taking for pain.

Medicine Name	Dose	Purpose of Medication	Side Effects

My Medications...

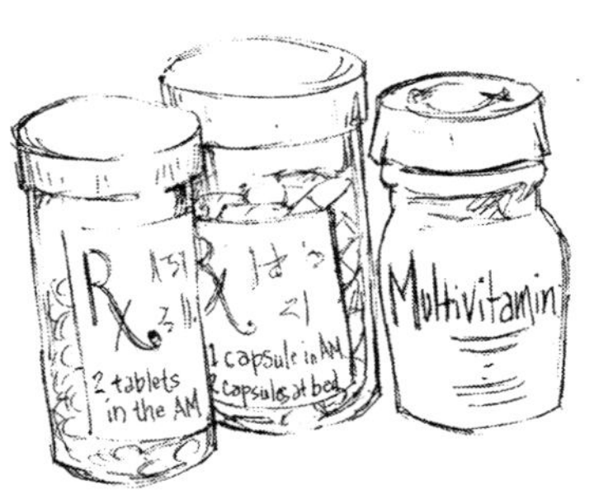

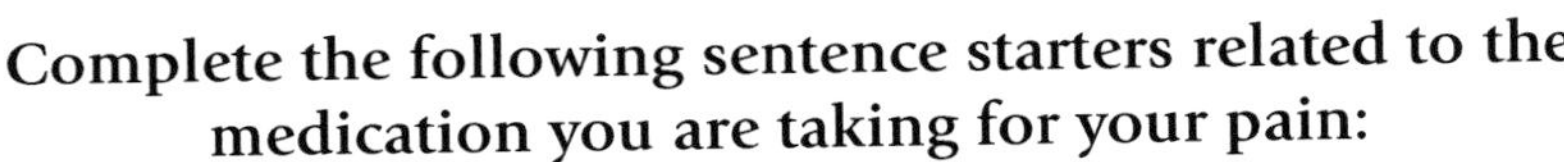

Complete the following sentence starters related to the medication you are taking for your pain:

The medications that make me feel better include ______________________________

____

The medications that do not seem to help are ______________________________

____

The medications negatively affect me by ______________________________

____

The side effects I have from taking medications include ______________________________

____

My different medications interfere with each other by ______________________________

____

I overuse medications by ______________________________

____

The concerns about the current medications I am taking include ______________________________

____

The medications I would like to try include ______________________________

____

My medications make me ______________________________

____

My medications reduce my ability to ______________________________

____

Instead of prescription medications I am using ______________________________

____

Other Ways I Relieve the Pain

Place a check in front of the items that you use to help relieve your pain. Next to each one that you've checked, describe how it works for you or doesn't.

- ❑ Acupuncture ____________________
- ❑ Aqua / Water Exercise ____________________
- ❑ Art Therapy ____________________
- ❑ Biofeedback ____________________
- ❑ Chiropractic ____________________
- ❑ Cranial Sacral ____________________
- ❑ Diet Therapy ____________________
- ❑ Exercises / Work-outs ____________________
- ❑ Guided Imagery / Visualization ____________________
- ❑ Heating Pad / Ice Pack / Hot / Cold Compresses ____________________
- ❑ Herbal remedies ____________________
- ❑ Homeopathy ____________________
- ❑ Humor Therapy ____________________
- ❑ Hypnosis ____________________
- ❑ Light Therapy ____________________
- ❑ Listening to Music ____________________
- ❑ Massage ____________________
- ❑ Meditation ____________________
- ❑ Music / Sound Therapy ____________________
- ❑ Non-Prescriptive Drugs ____________________
- ❑ Occupational Therapy ____________________
- ❑ Pet Therapy ____________________
- ❑ Physical Therapy ____________________
- ❑ Pilates, Qi Gong, Shiatsu or Tai Chi ____________________
- ❑ Prayer ____________________
- ❑ Recreation Therapy ____________________
- ❑ Yoga ____________________

Other ____________________

Now place a check AFTER the activities you would like to try.

My Pain...

Complete the following sentence starters related to the pain you are feeling:

My pain keeps me from ____

____

____

My pain gets worse when I ____

____

____

My pain affects my mood by ____

____

____

My pain affects my work by ____

____

____

My pain affects my relationships by ____

____

____

My pain dissipates when I ____

____

____

My pain causes me other problems such as ____

____

____

My pain is caused from ____

____

____

A Pain Quotation

> *Pain is such an uncomfortable feeling*
> *that even a tiny amount of it is enough*
> *to ruin every enjoyment.*
>
> ~ **Will Rogers**

What does this quote mean to you? ______________________________

____

____

____

____

What types of pain do you experience? ______________________________

____

____

____

How does your pain ruin your enjoyment in life? ______________________________

____

____

____

What activities can you no longer enjoy because of your pain? ______________________________

____

____

____

____

My Pain-Free Journal

This is your pain-free page. Write words of your own, uplifting spiritual sayings or quotes, or paste photographs or pictures from magazines, that remind you that you can triumph over your pain! Post it in a visible place to keep you motivated.

Whole Person Associates is the leading publisher of training resources for professionals who empower people to create and maintain healthy lifestyles. Our creative resources will help you work effectively with your clients in the areas of stress management, wellness promotion, mental health and life skills.

Please visit us at our web site: **www.wholeperson.com**. You can check out our entire line of products, place an order, request our print catalog, and sign up for our monthly special notifications.

Whole Person Associates

800-247-6789